ROCKFORD PUBLIC LIBRARY
Rockford, Illinois
www.rockfordpubliclibrary.org
815-965-9511

FORENSIC SCIENCE INVESTIGATED

CAREERS | IN FORENSICS

WRITTEN BY:
Linda D. Williams

mc Marshall Cavendish
Benchmark
New York

MARSHALL CAVENDISH BENCHMARK
99 WHITE PLAINS ROAD
TARRYTOWN, NEW YORK 10591-9001
www.marshallcavendish.us

LIBRARY OF CONGRESS CATALOGING-IN-PUBLICATION DATA
Williams, Linda D.
Careers in forensics / by Linda D. Williams.
p. cm. — (Forensic science investigated)
Includes bibliographical references and index.
ISBN 978-0-7614-3080-3
1. Forensic sciences—Vocational guidance—Juvenile literature.
2. Criminal investigation—Juvenile literature. I. Title.
HV8073.8.W55 2009
363.325023—dc22
2008003627

EDITOR: Christina Gardeski   PUBLISHER: Michelle Bisson
ART DIRECTOR: Anahid Hamparian   SERIES DESIGNER: Kristen Branch
Photo Research by Anne Burns Images

Cover Photo by Corbis/Andrew Brookes Back Cover Photo by Phototake/Terry Why

The photographs in this book are used with permission and through the courtesy of:
iStockphoto: pp. 1, 3 (hand Chris Hutchinson, cells David Marchal). Alamy: p. 4 louise
murray; p. 7 Alex Segre; p. 39 Arthur Turner; p. 58 SHOUT; pp. 61, 71 Mikael Karlsson.
Corbis: p. 10 Bettman; p. 17 Anna Clopet; p. 22 Keith Dannemiller; p. 26 Jim Craigmyle;
p. 28 Ed Young; p. 37 Najlah Feanny/SABA; p. 43 Shepard Sherbell/SABA; p. 48 Horacio
Villalobos; pp. 57, 74 Reuters; p. 76 William Whitehurst; p. 78 Ramin Talaie; p. 80 Andrew
Brookes. Getty Images: pp. 12, 63; p. 68 Time & Life Pictures. Photo Researchers: pp. 20,
52, 64 Michael Donne; p. 40 Dr. Jurgen Scriba. Associated Press: pp. 33, 88.

Printed in Malaysia
1 3 5 6 4 2

Cover: A forensic scientist tests evidence.

CONTENTS

Collection of a soil sample from a suspect's boot

WHAT IS FORENSICS?

AN OLD MAN DIES when his house burns down. It looks like a tragic accident—until investigators find traces of an **accelerant,** a substance that can be used to start fires or make them burn hotter and faster. Police then discover that the old man's nephew, who would have gotten the money from his uncle's life insurance policy, recently bought a large container of the accelerant.

A hit-and-run driver strikes a boy on a bicycle. The car leaves a few tiny flakes of paint on the boy's clothes and the mangled frame of his bike. The bits of paint are so small that they are almost invisible to the unaided eye, but they are enough to lead police to the car and the guilty driver.

"My wife just shot herself!" a man cries out to the operator at the emergency 911 number. Deputies from the sheriff's office find the dead woman slumped in a chair with a shotgun in her hands. They make a detailed photographic record of the scene. A crime scene specialist reviews the photographs and reports that the evidence does not match the husband's story. According to the size and shape of the blood spatters on the wall behind the chair, the woman was shot from ten feet away, while she was standing up. Why would the husband lie? There is only one reason: he murdered his wife—but drops of her blood had pointed to the truth.

Each of these cases was solved with the help of **forensic science**, which is the use of scientific methods and tools to investigate crimes and bring suspects to trial. The term "forensic" comes from ancient Rome, where people debated matters of law in a public meeting place called the Forum. The Latin word *forum* gave rise to *forensic*, meaning "relating to courts of law or to public debate." Today the term **forensics** has several meanings. One is the art of speaking in debates, which is why some schools have forensics clubs or teams for students who want to learn debating skills. The best-known meaning of "forensics," though, is crime solving through forensic science.

Fascination with forensics explains the popularity of many recent TV shows, movies, and books, but

▲ The ruins of the Roman Forum

crime and science have been linked for a long time. The first science used in criminal investigation was medicine, and one of the earliest reports of forensic medicine comes from ancient Rome. In 44 BCE, the Roman leader Julius Caesar was stabbed to death not far from the Forum. A physician named Antistius examined the body and found that Caesar had received twenty-three stab wounds, but only one wound was fatal.

Antistius had performed one of history's first recorded **postmortem** examinations, in which a physician looks at a body to find out how the person died. But forensics has always had limits. Antistius could point out the chest wound that had killed Caesar, but he could not say who had struck the deadly blow.

Death in its many forms inspired the first forensic manuals. The oldest one was published in China in 1248. Called *Hsi duan yu* (The Washing Away of Wrongs), it tells of differences between the bodies of people who have been strangled and drowning victims. When a corpse is recovered from the water, says the manual, officers of the law should examine the tissues and small bones in the neck. Torn tissues and broken bones show that the victim met with foul play before being thrown into the water.

Poison became another landmark in the history of forensics in 1813, when Mathieu Orfila, a professor of medical and forensic chemistry at the University of Paris, published *Traité des poisons* (A Treatise on Poisons). Orfila described the deadly effects of various mineral, vegetable, and animal substances. He laid the foundation of the modern science of **toxicology,** the branch of forensics that deals with poisons, drugs, and their effects on the human body.

As France's most famous expert on poisons, Orfila played a part in an 1840 criminal trial that received wide publicity. Marie LaFarge was accused of murder after the death of her husband. Orfila testified that he had examined the husband's corpse and found arsenic in the body. LaFarge insisted that she had not fed the arsenic to her husband and that he must have eaten it while away from home. The court, however, sentenced her to life imprisonment. Pardoned in 1850 after ten years in prison, LaFarge died the next year, proclaiming her innocence to the end.

Cases such as the LaFarge trial highlighted the growing use of medical evidence in criminal investigations and trials. Courts were recognizing other kinds of forensic evidence, too. In 1784 a British murder case had been decided by physical evidence. The torn edge of a piece of newspaper found in the pocket of a suspect named John Toms matched the torn edge of a ball of paper found in the pistol thought to have been used to fire the fatal head shot. At the time, people used rolled pieces of cloth or paper, called wadding, to hold bullets firmly in gun barrels. Toms was declared guilty of murder. In 1835 an officer of Scotland Yard, Britain's famous police division, caught a murderer by using a flaw on the fatal bullet to trace the bullet to its maker. Such cases marked the birth of **ballistics**, the branch of forensics that deals with firearms.

▲ Outside Scotland Yard Hall, London

Not all forensic developments involved murder. Science also helped solve crimes such as arson and forgery. By the early nineteenth century, chemists had developed the first tests to identify certain dyes used in ink. Experts could then determine the age and chemical makeup of the ink on documents, such as wills and valuable manuscripts, that were suspected of being fakes.

Forensics started to become a regular part of police work at the end of the nineteenth century, after an Austrian law professor named Hans Gross published a two-volume handbook on the subject in 1893. Gross's book, usually referred to in English-speaking countries as *Criminal Investigation*, brought together all the many techniques that scientists and law enforcers had developed for examining the physical evidence of crime—bloodstains, bullets, and more. Police departments started using *Criminal Investigation* to train officers. The book entered law school courses as well.

Modern forensics experts regard Hans Gross as the founder of their profession. Among other contributions, Gross coined the word **criminalistics**. He used the term to refer to the general study of crime or criminals. Today, however, "criminalistics" has a narrower, more specific meaning. It refers to the study of physical evidence from crime scenes.

Almost every branch of science has been involved in criminal investigations. Meteorologists have testified about the weather on the date of a crime. Botanists have named the plants that produced tiny specks of pollen found on suspects' clothes. Dentists have matched bite marks on victims' bodies to killers' teeth. Criminalistics—the collecting, protecting, and examining of crime scene evidence—is the basis for these and other forms of forensic investigation. Whether they are called criminalists, crime scene investigators (CSIs), or scene-of-crime officers (SOCOs), the men and women who work with the physical and biological signs of crime are the first to give the evidence a chance to speak—to reveal what really happened.

Preparing blood
samples for evidence
in a crime lab

CHAPTER ONE

IS FORENSICS FOR YOU?

▼ SO YOU THINK SCIENCE IS COOL,

but you don't see yourself teaching or doing equations all day. What are your options?

Guidance counselors and skill tests reveal that you are a rational thinker, able to come up with creative ideas. You could work in an art gallery as well as a scientific field. Medicine might be interesting, but you wonder whether you have the skills or patience to listen to people talk about their aches and pains all day. Which careers will hold your attention and stay challenging?

Finding work that continually presents different questions and scenarios can be a tall order. However, there are a number of career options in a field that is perfectly suited to someone whose creative mind loves to investigate and experiment: forensic science. According to the National Institutes of Health's Office of Science Education, people who like a feeling of accomplishment, using technical skills, and scheduling their own work activities with little supervision will find that forensic science can keep them interested for years.

Forensic science includes any scientific field used to explain evidence in legal proceedings. Forensics uncovers exact information about the evidence of a crime. Well-tested and well-defined evidence provides clues to what actually took place at a crime scene. Something that many of us wouldn't notice, like a stray hair on an armchair or a worn place on a window frame, can be used by investigators and law enforcement personnel to figure out the how, when, where, and who of a crime. The "why" is a job for the psychologists, attorneys, accountants, and the judicial system.

Forensics draws upon strong scientific skills combined with a keen sense of detail and stubborn determination to find answers. As with any science, a person interested in entering forensic work must never be satisfied with the obvious or first impression of a crime scene. Like the fictional detective Sherlock Holmes, a criminalist must observe the smallest of details and catalog everything. What seems unimportant at first may, during the course of an investigation, be the key to solving a crime or identifying a victim.

▶ TRAINING AND SKILLS

Crime scene investigators collect material evidence from crime scenes, victims, and suspects. They turn this evidence over to forensic scientists to examine for clues that might be able to help in a given investigation. Forensic specialists generally work closely with police, since the investigation is an important step in the discovery of what happened and in any subsequent legal proceedings. In fact, forensic specialists often visit crime scenes and testify in court as expert witnesses.

Criminal investigators do more than identify, document, and collect evidence. A key part of their job is to reconstruct the different components of a crime. They must be able to use educational training, intuition, and documented evidence to piece a crime scene puzzle back together.

First, however, a person interested in forensics or crime scene investigation must study to become proficient at recognizing clues. As any expert knows, some things are black and white, but there are gray areas of science that must be tested from different angles to get the best answer. Learning how to make scientific and ethical decisions is very important, especially when test results could mean life or death for an accused suspect.

Criminalists usually have a four-year degree in forensic science, criminalistics, biology, chemistry, physics, or other science, depending on the program. A minor in chemistry is usually required, and many people go on to complete advanced degrees. Training can be obtained on the job or in specialized courses offered at criminalistics schools, through the Federal Bureau of Investigation (FBI) or the Bureau of Alcohol, Tobacco, Firearms and Explosives (ATF), or through some universities.

Anyone interested in forensic science needs to load up on science and mathematics courses in high school to prepare for a college or university program in forensic science, criminalistics, physics, biology, or engineering. After college, application to a state, county, or city forensics office is common, since most crime laboratories are managed by government agencies. The hiring process can take up to six months because an extensive background check is an important part of the process. Forensic investigators cannot have any misdemeanor or felony convictions.

As with other technical fields, a student internship in a crime, toxicology, or pathology laboratory helps make the daily work understandable. Experience and skills gained during an internship are useful later when it's necessary to recognize clues, make decisions, and collect **trace evidence** for testing.

Specialty training for specific segments of criminal investigations can be completed at institutions such as the FBI Academy located on the U.S. Marine Corps Base at Quantico, Virginia. Since 1972, the Quantico facility has been the site of extensive FBI training as well as Drug Enforcement Administration (DEA) training. In addition to classrooms and a forensic science research and training center, the complex includes dormitories, indoor and outdoor firing ranges, skeet ranges, and a rifle range.

▲ Cadets perform a mock arrest during a training exercise at the FBI Academy in Quantico, Virginia.

Quantico's Investigative Computer Training Unit (ICTU) provides investigative computer instruction, training, and curriculum development to FBI recruits, FBI agents, FBI professional support staff, and domestic and international law enforcement officers. Training includes using a computer as an investigative, research, and analytical tool for examining digital evidence.

Research done at the academy in the areas of DNA analysis, biochemistry, chemistry, and physics focuses on developing or improving methods for the analysis of forensic evidence. Researchers from academia, private industry, and other government laboratories, as well as state and local forensic laboratories, work together.

▶ CHOOSING A SPECIALTY

One of the things people entering forensic fields like about their jobs is that the work can be tailored to fit individual interests. The most important characteristics a person needs in a forensic career are curiosity and an investigative nature.

Many people think that a job in forensics is largely centered on police work and lab analyses. This is partially true, but forensics touches on anything that will be presented in a court of law. So the variety of applicable job skills and available careers is broad. You don't even have to like labs to find interesting work in the world of forensic investigation. Accountants, nurses, doctors, anthropologists, dentists, engineers, psychologists, photographers, and artists are among the many professionals who have concentrated their careers on forensics. With special training and education, the number of jobs related to the scientific examination, legal analysis, and prosecution of criminal cases are plentiful.

Income in the forensic sciences varies according to education level, job, location, and the number of hours worked. Although such a career is not a sure path to riches, forensic investigators and scientists make a good living. Besides salary, which can vary from a median annual wage of $39,200 for technicians in Texas to between $35,000 and $47,000 for technicians in California, forensics provides job satisfaction not easily gained elsewhere. Job experience and numbers of hours worked affect these salary amounts as well.

As in many jobs, the more education and experience a person has, the higher the salary. Depending upon the job, forensic scientists work various hours. Some work a forty-hour week with weekends off, while others work in the field on different schedules and may be "on call." Nearly every area of forensic science offers chances for career advancement and salary growth.

One way to choose a specialty in forensic science is to think of all the places and details involved in the investigation of a crime or disaster. These can be outside, on

▲ A scene-of-crime officer (SOCO) photographs evidence collected from a fire.

land, in air and water, or inside a private home or a public location like a hotel, restaurant, mall, or airport.

Some forensic specialists, such as forensic photographers and artists, can do their jobs in almost any location. However, other jobs are tied to an external location, such as the study of vehicle skid marks, taillight fragments, a felled tree, or footprints in soil. Finding fingerprints is more often an inside task, since investigators can find fingerprints on countertops, stair rails, and drinking glasses. Thinking about where different forensic tasks are usually performed might help narrow your search for a specialty, depending on whether you enjoy the outdoors or prefer air conditioning.

Scientists rely on technology to help them gather and analyze information. The education or experience needed for a particular forensic science career depends on the level of technical analysis involved.

Forensic botanists, experts in various plants and seeds, have an education similar to that of a research biologist, but focused primarily on **botany.** The appropriate college science and mathematics classes include beginning biology, genetics, algebra, calculus, and physics—and, of course, enough credits in plant structure and physiology to constitute a major in botany.

The expertise of a forensic botanist is often important in understanding where a crime was committed.

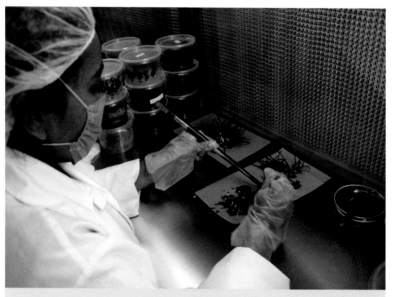

▲ A botanist examines and stores plants in specimen jars.

For example, if a corpse is found in the trunk of an abandoned car at a truck stop, police will want to know whether the murder was committed at the truck stop or elsewhere. Dried brambles found in the hair or clothes of the victim during autopsy may offer a clue. After examining a bramble under a microscope, a forensic botanist might find that the specific strain of bramble in the sample grows only in a geographical area several hundred miles from the truck stop. This information gives investigators a possible murder location and a place to look for more clues or possible witnesses.

What of people particularly interested in **DNA (deoxyribonucleic acid)** who want to become DNA experts? Students should complete the college science classes such as biology and chemistry to get a good grasp of the subject, along with on-the-job technical experience. This training becomes important in quickly recognizing whether a DNA sample is from a human or animal source.

When violence is suspected in modern investigations, blood, other body fluids, and hair samples are collected from the body for DNA and protein analysis. Blood from a victim or crime scene is tested to find out which of four broad groups it belongs to: O, A, B, or AB. The result is compared against a suspect's blood type to determine whether there is a match. Sometimes, a blood type is found that doesn't belong to anyone known to be connected with the crime. When this happens, forensic scientists notify their supervisors that the investigation is not complete because others may be involved.

To be considered a DNA expert and offer expert testimony in a courtroom, a forensic scientist must not only be able to do DNA and protein analyses, but also compare different DNA typing techniques, explain different uses of DNA typing, and identify possible pluses and minuses of DNA typing during a trial.

The same is true of chemistry or toxicology. There are standard science and mathematics classes that every chemistry major must take. These include fundamentals of chemistry, organic and inorganic chemistry, analytical chemistry, physical chemistry, physics, statistics, algebra, and calculus. Specialists also learn how to perform chemical screening analyses in a toxicology lab. Results from these tests are essential in cases involving drugs, poisoning, toxic waste, and many other areas.

▶ LABORATORY ASSIGNMENTS AND CONSULTANCIES

If you are particularly interested in laboratory work, there are usually two styles of daily activity. In the first, forensic scientists do one type of analysis throughout their career. In the second, science personnel are shifted around to various laboratory assignments, which broadens their experience and expertise. Additionally, some labs ask personnel to go to a crime scene, collect data, and then return to the lab to analyze it, while others have criminalists send samples back to the lab for analysis.

In a forensic lab, chemists, pathologists, immunologists, and serologists use a variety of instruments, depending on the evidence. Such equipment includes ultraviolet (UV) spectrometers, which measure the absorbance of UV and visible light in determining a sample's chemical properties; infrared (IR) spectrometers, which use light of specific wavelengths to discover chemical structure; and finally, gas chromatograph-mass spectrometers (GC-MS), which are used in separating compounds in a mixture. This equipment helps to identify the composition of trace evidence samples and provide investigators with clues.

Serving as a forensic consultant or expert witness provides another exciting and often well-paid career path option. This kind of work, which allows greater independence in scheduling daily activities, has the added benefit of allowing one to be self-employed. Expert consultants may work for contract service organizations (CSOs) or establish their own certified forensic labs.

▶ TEAMWORK

No matter what specialty a person chooses, teamwork is a big part of forensic investigation. In addition to concentrating on their individual work, every member of a forensic team must also become integrated into a larger community of investigators. As all the various clues in a case are brought together, patterns and connections begin to appear.

Everyone on the team must have good communication skills, both verbal and written. Each member must also learn to value every other investigator's input, because each area of an investigation is important to the overall solving of a case. Think of an investigation

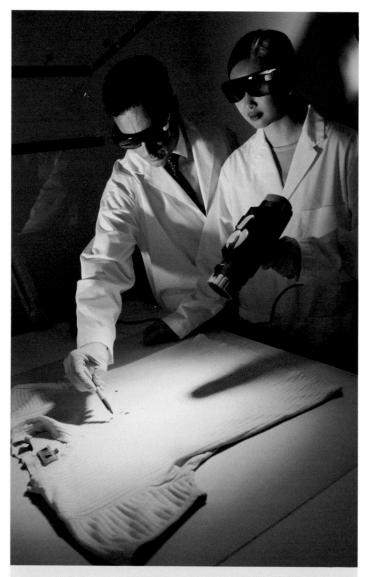

▲ Scientists use a forensic light source to examine evidence.

as being like your body. Just because you enjoy doing things with your hands doesn't make your feet or your heart any less important. Each has its own job to do for the entire body to work efficiently. Also, as in the body, all the specialists participating in an investigation are not needed for every activity. For example, when your mouth and tongue are hard at work during a meal or conversation, your legs and feet may be at rest.

It is the same for members of a forensic team. Depending on the circumstances of an investigation, a forensic geologist or ballistics expert might discover the key clue to solving the case, while a handwriting or computer expert may not be needed. During another case, however, such as a bank fraud or counterfeiting case, these team members would play a key role.

Just as there are many potential career paths available in forensics, there are different levels of experience, certification, and education (bachelor's, master's, and doctoral degrees) that make it possible for people from backgrounds and interests of all kinds to work together in solving crimes.

Realizing that you are just one person in a bigger picture is the first step in becoming an excellent forensic investigator. Additionally, the knowledge and understanding that the overall picture changes with each case keeps forensic work fresh.

An entomologist
performs research in
a lab.

CHAPTER TWO

THE NATURAL AND MEDICAL SCIENCES

▼ THE NATURAL SCIENCES DEAL WITH

living organisms and the natural world's contents: ecosystems, lakes, streams, geological formations, and so on. In criminal investigations, the natural sciences in practice are primarily biology and chemistry. These scientific fields look at the inner workings of living systems and their internal composition. When such a system is disrupted through an accident or violence, the extent of the damage to it is assessed by comparison to a similar healthy system.

Forensic biologists and chemists often specialize in a particular area. They may perform graduate research in a college or university lab or apply to programs offering advanced criminal investigative education such as the John Jay College of Criminal Justice at the City University of New York.

A forensic biologist could be a botanist who studies plants, a zoologist who studies animals, a microbiologist who focuses on bacteria and viruses, or an entomologist who studies insects. Other forensic microbiologists include research mycologists or parasitologists, who study fungi and parasites.

Forensic chemists play a crucial role in the specific analysis of solid, liquid, and gaseous substances discovered during the course of a criminal investigation. They may specialize in molecular biology, biochemistry, or toxicology to gain deeper insight into the structure and functionality of a substance.

Future forensic chemists pursue the standard undergraduate chemistry curriculum offered at major universities. Since the field is broad, most graduates pursue advanced degrees such as master of science or doctoral degrees, which call for two to six additional years of training. To specialize in forensic science, chemists must complete one to three more years of training designed to impart an expert understanding of reactions between compounds and the role they may have played in a crime. Depending on the circumstances, any number of combinations of the natural and medical sciences and other forensic areas might be needed to solve a crime or untangle a disaster.

▶ THE LOST AIRMEN

When a dead man was discovered in a rock glacier by a backpacker in the Sierra Nevada Mountains in August 2007, forensic anthropologists were flown in to recover the body. The Fresno County Coroner's Office, which was overseeing retrieval of the remains, also collected a nearby parachute.

The body had been located in approximately the same area as another man's body, found in October 2005 on a glacier in Kings Canyon National Park. These earlier remains were identified as those of army airman Leo Mustonen. Mustonen and three others never returned from an AT-7 navigational flight that had taken off from an airfield in Sacramento, California, on November 18, 1942.

The recently discovered remains, suspected to be from the same downed plane from the World War II era, were found in the rock layer, whereas the 2005 body had been encased in ice.

THE INVESTIGATION BEGINS

A variety of information had to be gathered to identify the newly discovered remains and determine the whereabouts of the rest of the crew and the airplane. When forensic anthropologists first arrived at the scene, photos were taken from several angles and distances in an effort to capture the scene exactly. Land contours and surrounding geography were noted for use by military experts in calculating the aircraft's trajectory as it went down. Details of the overall location were carefully recorded and compared with the site at which the first airman's body was found.

Everything that belonged to the dead man found in 2007 was carefully removed from the site and labeled with identification numbers. The time, date, and location of each article were also recorded. Since the body and scene had been exposed to the elements for sixty-five years, trace evidence had mixed with snow, dirt, twigs, and insects. Animals in the area may have disturbed the site as well.

The remains were sent to Hickam Air Force Base in Hawaii, where army experts in several fields proceeded with the identification process.

Insect populations allow forensic entomologists to narrow down the window of time in which death probably occurred, a key factor in homicide investigations.

▲ Insects collected from a crime scene

A decomposing body usually contains several types of fly larvae, or maggots, along with beetles and a few centipedes. Time of death may be determined from the number and variety of these inhabitants, since different insects appear during decomposition at different times. Some flies arrive within a few minutes while larger beetles may not show up for twenty-four hours. So, a sampling of insects from the body, along with photos and notes of where they were collected, are sent to a forensic entomologist for study. Although the date of the crash is known, circumstances right after the crash are still a mystery. These may be gained from study of the insect evidence.

If the body had not been encased in ice, it would have been compared with decomposition information available from the body farms, research facilities in Tennessee and North Carolina. These facilities make it possible for forensic anthropologists, medical examiners, and police detectives to better understand the process of human body decomposition during various conditions—under a hot sun, for example, buried in a shallow grave in damp soil, or left for long periods in the trunks of vehicles during different seasonal climates. Hot and dry desert climates delay insect arrival and bacterial decomposition. Extreme cold tends to slow or suspend decomposition long enough for tissues to freeze-dry and mummify. Forensic odontologists also compared the dental records of the lost airmen with the teeth and dental structure of the recovered body.

A forensic chemist performed biochemical testing on body tissues to look for unexpected substances. Trace contaminants would include poisons, drugs, alcohol, and any cellular damage not consistent with obvious external injuries. Chemical tests of the airman's clothes or skin for traces of airplane fuel could provide more information about the crash.

ADDITIONAL TESTS

During the course of the study, forensic pathologists and technicians used specialized microscopes to examine the collected samples. These included polarized-light microscopes to examine glass crystals and parachute and clothing fibers; dark-field microscopes, which use scattered light to reveal tiny bits of debris; and phase-contrast microscopes, which allow investigators to distinguish substances in the samples that differ in their chemical composition.

Forensic geologists may attempt to recreate the circumstances of how the airman's body came to be lying more than a hundred feet from Mustonen's body. Several possibilities might be discussed in terms of the topography of the area. For example, did the airman survive the initial impact and attempt to pull himself clear of the crash site, fearing an explosion? If and when the airplane is finally found, more clues may be available to help solve the mystery.

Forensic results will either help prove or disprove the circumstances surrounding the airman's identity and death. Military investigators hope to positively identify the airman and learn more about the circum-stances of his death.

▶ MEDICAL SCIENCES

Forensic medical science professionals, such as pathologists, medical examiners, serologists, immunologists, DNA analysts, and odontologists, work primarily on victims' and suspects' identities, also trying to determine times and causes of death. They serve as expert, living witnesses in a court of law, testifying on evidence from the tissue and cellular levels that points to how a victim died. Identifying the dead is an important job of forensic medical scientists. Bringing closure to investigations, as well as friends and relatives, is a top priority. As in the cases of the missing airmen, even years after their deaths, identification is still possible with current technology.

DOCTORS

To become a physician requires completion of four years of college in a science or premedical curriculum, followed by four years of medical school. Many people think that after graduating from medical school with an MD degree, a doctor's education is finished. Fortunately for patients, this is only the first part of a physician's training. To specialize in a certain area of interest such as pathology, a person who has obtained an MD degree

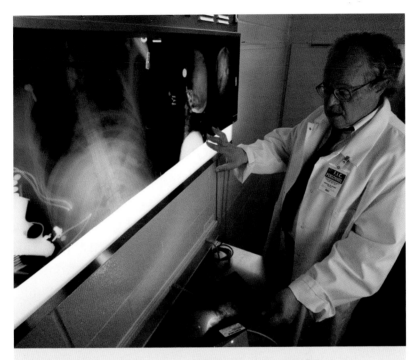

▲ A doctor examines an X-ray containing a gun, bullets, lungs, and a skull.

will often be required to complete another two to six years of residency education in a hospital setting, closely supervised by senior physicians. Once a certain level of achievement has been attained and medical certification examinations passed, the physician is ready to gain experience in forensic medicine if he or she chooses.

In general, while many doctors fight disease and take care of the living, forensic pathologists and medical examiners serve the dead. A **medical examiner (ME)** is a physician who is authorized by a governmental agency to investigate the cause of sudden or unusual deaths by examining human remains. A pathologist is a doctor who performs autopsies and examines tissue samples to elicit information on how a person died.

SEROLOGISTS

The scientific study of the properties and interactions of bodily fluids (blood, semen, saliva, sweat, urine, or feces) is known as **serology**. Blood evidence is often present at the scenes of violent crimes such as homicide and assault. Investigators find everything from tiny droplets to large pools of blood. Blood can be liquid, clotted, or dried. The condition of blood evidence determines which of the available collection and testing methods will be used.

At first, a serologist can perform several tests on a stain suspected to be blood. A visual inspection is the easiest, since blood is most often bright red or brown. Also, depending on the scene, the victim's body or a murder weapon may be nearby. A Kastle-Meyer test produces a pink to purple color and bubbling when chemicals come in contact with the iron in a blood sample. Some plant material contains iron as well, however, and this means that a positive Kastle-Meyer test calls for further investigation.

BLOODSTAIN PATTERNS

JOHN GLAISTER JR. (1892–1971), wrote extensively about bloodstains in the 1930s, and his classifications are still used today. Glaister had three categories of bloodstains: passive, such as those droplets falling onto a surface due to gravity; transfer, from a bloody object pulled across a surface; and projected, describing stains that occur when blood spatters upon impact or sprays from a wound at different angles.

Bloodstain patterns are often used by crime scene investigators to determine direction, distance, velocity, and course of events. Blood splatter patterns can show whether a fatal wound was made by a bullet, for example, or by another means, such as a knife. Moreover, pooled blood at a crime scene lets police know that a victim lived at least briefly after a fatal wound, since the heart was still beating, causing the blood to flow. Death stops the heart, and therefore blood flow, so when a corpse is found with serious wounds but very little blood, it is likely that the body was moved from the original crime scene.

Bloodstain patterns are very important in violent crimes. Depending on the height and angle of a blood spatter on a wall, a defendant might be found guilty of murder instead of self-defense.

• • • • •

A STAGED MURDER SCENE WITH BLOODSTAINS ON A FLOOR WITH BULLET CASINGS

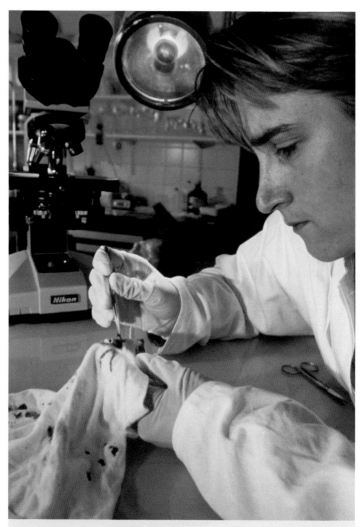

▲ A forensic scientist removes a fragment of material, from which to extract a blood sample, from a bloodstained garment recovered from a crime scene.

To determine whether a stain contains human blood, serologists use a precipitin test. They add the crime scene sample to a control substance that contains human-specific blood proteins and binding chemicals that will form white clumps upon contact with blood from a person. Different proteins and chemicals are used to identify different types of animal blood. Once blood is found to be human, Landsteiner's system of blood typing is used to include or exclude possible suspects as contributing to the crime.

IMMUNOLOGISTS

Forensic immunologists study the immune system. They research how the human body reacts to attack by various substances, present perhaps in tiny amounts. To become a research immunologist, a person would study biology in college and then pursue graduate studies in immunology. A physician might choose a residency with a focus on the human immune system and how infections and terminal disease affect it.

The goal of a forensic immunologist is to discover whether the immune system under investigation was affected by natural degradation or fell victim to poisons or an infectious disease such as anthrax. Specific analytical and often toxicological testing must be done to determine whether death was the result of immune system collapse.

PATHOLOGISTS

An **autopsy**, also known as a postmortem examination, is done by a medical doctor called a pathologist under a number of circumstances. Examples include the following: death that occurs suddenly within twenty-four hours of admittance to a hospital or of a surgical procedure; the body is to be cremated, dissected, or buried at sea; death under suspicious circumstances; employment-related death; death occurring in a psychiatric institution or prison; when a threat exists to public health; or when criminal violence is suspected. An autopsy is a medical procedure in which a corpse is examined to find the cause and manner of death, as well as any injuries or disease that was present at the time of death.

When facial features are not preserved well or have been too badly damaged to make a positive identification, pathologists must look for birthmarks, tattoos, piercings, or old scars, in addition to recent injuries. Since each person's life experiences are unique, even identical twins may carry different scars from childhood—perhaps one had a knee surgery and the other didn't.

The body is then x-rayed to look for recent broken bones or evidence of old injuries that might help in the identification process. For example, when a bone

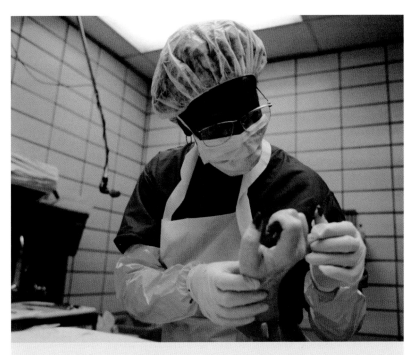

▲ A medical examiner performs an autopsy.

breaks, a hematoma, or bruise, is formed around it. A clot forms over the area, followed by the formation of a mass of fibrous tissue called a callus. The callus grows and hardens, becoming new bone that helps knit the broken bone back together. Over time, new bone fills in and the body's structure becomes solid again.

Besides looking at bones, an autopsy includes the examination of thin samples taken from different tissues and organs. These samples are studied by a pathologist under a high-powered microscope to look for tiny clues to trauma, time, or cause of death.

Rigor mortis is the term that describes changes that take place after death, when the body's muscles slowly stiffen and become rigid as a result of chemical changes. Rigor usually starts about three to four hours after death, with full rigidity occurring in about twelve hours. Temperature and degree of physical activity immediately before death affect these time estimates. What most people don't know is that rigor eventually disappears, and after about seventy-two hours, the remains have lost their stiffness. For forensic investigators, rigor mortis provides only a means of estimating time of death, not an exact time.

Since blood stops circulating after death, gravity causes it to pool in the lowermost tissues. At autopsy, a body found lying face up has blood pooled at the back of the head, shoulders, buttocks, calves, and heels. A big clue to investigators that a body was moved after death would be autopsy findings that blood was not pooled as it would have been if the person had died in the place and position in which the body was found.

DNA ANALYSTS

Since 1953, when James Watson, Francis Crick, and Maurice Wilkins unveiled their model of the structure and function of DNA, forensic scientists have been interested in using components of this essential protein as a type of "genetic fingerprint."

In modern investigations, DNA experts analyze blood, body fluids, and hair samples taken from the body when violence is suspected. Samples may also be collected from skin cells found under a victim's fingernails. Blood contains certain protein factors that show whether a person has blood types O, A, B, or AB. These could help either convict or acquit a suspect in the case based on whether their blood type or DNA profile was found at the scene or upon the victim. In fact, there have been some cases where a suspect was arrested for a crime, but then released, after a DNA analyst checked the suspect's DNA samples against those from the victim and scene and determined they did not match the suspect.

If the flesh of a body has decomposed completely or beyond any chance of recognition, the bones must be x-rayed, and DNA analysis and dental record study must be performed. DNA results are compared against samples of relatives' DNA to see whether the similarities are great enough to be called, loosely, "a match." If police think they know who the victim is, but can't tell from a visual examination, they often use DNA taken from hair in a comb or brush known to have been used by the victim. DNA databases on military personnel and prison inmates can also be checked, although access to this information is granted only to authorized investigators.

The great strides made in DNA analysis in the past twenty years cannot be emphasized enough. In fact, most criminalists and forensic experts believe that the field will continue to grow in importance. With broader DNA databases, DNA collected from crime scenes will become the single most important category of evidence about victims and perpetrators alike.

Large metropolitan laboratories are using extremely advanced DNA typing methods. Costs are dropping, and confidence that the results obtained will stand up in court is increasing. However, it will be some time before all these excellent techniques are used routinely in smaller or rural labs.

Discussions are ongoing about whether DNA samples should be collected from every person. Although this would make forensic investigation easier when an identification has yet to be made, many people fear that the information could fall into the wrong hands. Most likely, the debate will continue, especially as DNA analysis becomes ever more accurate.

ANTHROPOLOGISTS

When a body is found a long time after death, there are often only bones and teeth remaining.

Nevertheless, bones can provide much information, such as the approximate age, height, weight, sex, and race of a victim. These clues are discovered by forensic anthropologists using their knowledge of bone development.

A forensic anthropologist can determine whether a skeleton was male or female depending on the width and shape of the hip bones. Men have narrow pelvic openings while women, genetically programmed to bear children, have open hips and wider pelvic openings. In addition, males have thicker, backward-sloping skulls, squarer chins, and thicker ridge bones above the eyes than women. Women's skulls show more rounded foreheads and chins and smooth bone about the eyes. Men usually have much broader shoulders than women and longer collarbones. If a skeleton is discovered to have both male (M) and female (F) traits, the anthropologist uses a mathematical equation to find the ratio of male characteristics to female traits. For example, a ratio of 15 M to 1 F would allow investigators to say that the bones are almost surely those of a male.

Anthropologists can also use bones to find a person's race. Race is manifested in differences between skull, teeth, and some body joint shapes. Some skeletons, of course, show a mixture of racial characteristics.

▲ Forensic anthropologists study bones to find clues used to solve crimes.

Once the race and sex of a skeleton have been identified, the focus turns to age. An anthropologist makes this determination from knowledge of several developmental bone changes that most humans experience. A baby or young child has around 300 separate bones that gradually grow together; the total count for adults is about 206 bones. In checking developmental age, anthropologists examine the bones of the skull (not completely solid until age forty), teeth, hips, joints, and ends of the collarbone, arm, and leg bones. Depending on the growth at these sites, a forensic anthropologist can distinguish among children, teens, young adults, and mature adults. In an older person, the body begins to lose bone mass and show signs of deterioration that are also indicators of age.

Height can be found by measuring the skeleton, but this is only a start. Depending on sex, race, and age, the amounts of tissue and cartilage between living bones can be very different. It is important to learn a victim's height during life because this is the number that will appear on the individual's official records. The best way for an anthropologist to find height is to measure a long bone and then apply a mathematical formula that considers all the variables of sex, age, and race.

Finding weight is more difficult. The fat cells of a decomposing body that has been buried in a moist place form a light brown, greasy film called **adipocere**. A body that has been underwater and relatively undisturbed for a long time forms so much adipocere that it is nearly impossible to state accurately how much the person weighed at the time of death. If no tissue is left on the bones, it is difficult for an anthropologist to determine the weight of a victim. Small ridges on the bones, indicating a strong muscle attachment, tell the trained observer that there had been more muscle mass than fat.

ODONTOLOGISTS

Another area of medical forensics is that of **odontology**, the study of dentistry and dental records for identification. When tissues and organs are no longer present to provide clues to identity or cause of death, and bones have little to offer besides overall size and sex of a person, a forensic odontologist studies the teeth in detail. In fact, the ancient Romans examined teeth for purposes of identification.

Very badly injured bodies, like those found burned in a plane crash or crushed in a building collapse, are extremely difficult to identify. Forensic odontologists are often called upon to compare dental records with the collected trace evidence. By comparing fillings, extractions, surface structure, neighboring teeth, and tilted teeth with known dental records or descriptions by family, the chances of making a match and providing positive identification are increased.

A scene-of-crime officer photographs a bullet hole in a pane of glass.

CHAPTER THREE

ENGINEERING AND
PHYSICS

▼ INVESTIGATORS TRAINED IN MANY

areas of engineering and physics can make the difference between solving a case and letting it become an unsolved mystery. These specialists examine evidence left behind at a crime scene that provides clues to the who, what, where, and how of a crime. For this reason, in addition to the investigators trained to identify unknown victims and possible suspects, others spend more time tracking objects and circumstances than checking on people. These investigators use engineering, physics, and computers to pinpoint how a crime was committed or why a disaster took place.

On September 11, 2001, the 110-story towers of the World Trade Center (WTC) in New York City were targeted by terrorists piloting commercial airliners. Unlike many crimes, these attacks were seen on television worldwide. The towers collapsed before the eyes of millions of horrified viewers. The death toll of identified people was nearly 2,800. Many more are thought to have died, but no physical evidence of their bodies has been found.

The forensic investigations of that crime were probably among the most extensive in the history of the United States. Because the terrorists' intent was death and destruction, the deaths were all considered to be homicides.

▶ ENGINEERS

Chemical engineers spent months trying to understand the sequence of events that led to the combustion, fires, and chemical reactions following the airliners' impacts into the towers. Even though jet fuel is extremely flammable, its role in causing damage within the steel structure is still a topic of debate among experts, since the actual sites of explosions inside the structure are not known.

Mechanical, structural, and electrical engineers also looked at the role of structural steel in the buildings' failure. They tried to project how the loads from destroyed sections may have precipitated the total collapse of each building. They considered the possibility that a different support configuration might have given the steel more strength under catastrophic loading. Their initial observations and later computer modeling became part of the criminal investigation of the 9/11 tragedy.

▶ ARSON EXPERTS

Crime scene investigations also often include arson, explosives, and ballistics experts. These technical investigators also use engineering, chemistry, and physics to figure out how a crime was committed.

When a 911 operator gets a call about an explosion and subsequent fire at an industrial building, firefighters are dispatched to the location immediately, along with police, to look for injured workers and to keep onlookers from getting too close. After the fire has been extinguished, an arson inspector carefully examines the burned scene for clues. Photographs are taken, people are interviewed, and evidence is collected.

An arson investigator is responsible for finding the origin, cause, and development of a fire, and whether the burning was achieved intentionally or was accidental. For example, when a house, public building, motor vehicle, aircraft, or other property is destroyed by fire and arson is suspected, an arson inspector tries to figure out how the crime was committed, and by whom.

THE WORLD TRADE CENTER COLLAPSE

THE DAMAGE TO THE WTC towers that resulted from the impacts of the commercial aircraft "was caused by the large mass of the aircraft, their high speed and momentum, which severed the relatively light steel of the exterior columns on the impact floors." This report came at the end of a three-year National Institute of Standards and Technology (NIST) investigation into the WTC towers collapse that included contributions from more than two hundred technical experts from the government, industry, and university settings. These experts examined thousands of documents, interviewed over a thousand people, reviewed 14,000 pieces of photographs and video segments, analyzed 236 steel wreckage fragments, and performed laboratory and computer simulations of aircraft impacts and building collapses.

NIST reported that the WTC towers collapsed because "(1) the impact of the planes severed and damaged support columns, dislodged fireproofing insulation coating the steel floor trusses and steel columns, and widely dispersed jet fuel over multiple floors; and (2) the subsequent unusually large amount of jet-fuel ignited multi-floor fires (with temperatures as high as 1,000 degrees Celsius), significantly weakening the floors and columns with dislodged fireproofing to the point where floors sagged and

THE RUBBLE OF THE TWIN TOWERS

pulled inward on the perimeter columns." The weakened structure was thought to have caused an inward bowing of the outside columns that initiated the towers' collapse.

NIST forensic engineers explained that the WTC steel structure did not melt from the heat, since the melting point of steel is about 1,500 degrees Celsius (roughly 2,800 degrees Fahrenheit). However, because the bare steel reached temperatures of 1,000 degrees Celsius (roughly 1,800 degrees Fahrenheit), it lost approximately 90 percent of its room-temperature strength. The steel, unprotected by the damaged fireproofing, was thought to have reached critical temperatures, which caused structural members to buckle and collapse.

· · · · ·

▲ Arson experts search for clues at the scene of a severe fire.

Determining the point where the first spark ignited usually is an indication of whether a fire was accidental or purposely set by an arsonist.

Arsonists often use accelerants like gasoline or turpentine to make a fire burn faster and hotter. Fires cannot burn without oxygen, fuel, and heat. If one of these factors is missing, the fire either won't start in the first place or will quickly go out. Arson investigators look for evidence that a destructive fire didn't start naturally and yet burned fiercely. Such a result points to the use of an accelerant.

Retardants slow down a fire. They're mostly used by firefighters, but sometimes an investigation reveals that an arsonist set a fire and then used a retardant to slow the blaze down while he escaped to establish an alibi.

One clue to a fire's origin is the direction and shape of a burn pattern. Fire, like heat, rises and spreads out away from the original spark point. If old wiring in a wall catches fire and burns, the flames will fan out as they get farther from the source, such as a wall switch. If there doesn't seem to be any cause of a spark, like lightning or an overheated circuit, experienced investigators know that something is not right. In such cases, they may look for accelerant chemicals that soaked into rugs and floors, and so were not completely used up in the fire. To pinpoint this kind of evidence, arson investigators use a "sniffer," such as a specially trained dog or sensitive monitoring instrument, to detect certain fumes from trace evidence.

▶ EXPLOSIVES EXPERTS

Experts who examine, study, and understand crime scenes or disasters involving explosives use methods similar to those of arson investigators. Usually they uncover some evidence of the type of explosive used. When a bomb detonates, pieces of **shrapnel** are blasted in all directions. Residue coats the crime scene. To prevent sample contamination and to minimize laboratory errors, inspectors carefully collect and store shrapnel in special plastic bags and metal containers.

After identifying an explosive, experts make blast area calculations to determine the amount of explosive used in a crime. These calculations include the blast extent and amount of damage. The amount of explosive used in multiple blasts and chain reaction blasts is difficult to determine.

▶ BALLISTICS EXPERTS

Ballistics experts study the trajectory or path of a **projectile** to help picture how a crime took place and the kind of weapon used. They test suspects and their clothing for gunpowder residue, mark the positions of empty cartridge cases, search the scene to account for every shot fired, reconstruct bullet trajectories, take photographs, and recover weapons.

When guns, bullets, or shell casings are found at a crime scene, experts compare them to bullets removed from walls, furniture, vehicles, or even a victim's body. Markings made by the ejector mechanism and weapon barrel in contact with the bullet during firing are unique to each weapon. When a gun is manufactured, it goes through a process called **rifling**, the cutting of spiral grooves into the interior of the gun's metal barrel. These grooves and lands (corresponding raised areas)

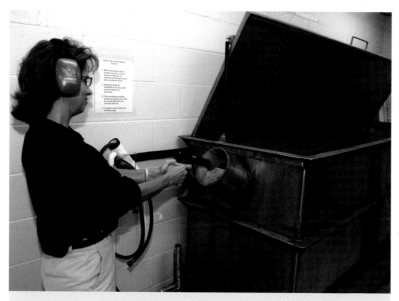

▲ A ballistics expert fires a gun into a water tank, then retrieves the bullet and compares it to bullets found at a crime scene.

created by rifling give bullets a stable spinning motion when they leave the gun barrel under pressure.

Every weapon type has a standard barrel length and diameter. So when ballistics experts examine the internal structure and rifling pattern of a weapon, they can figure out the caliber of bullet that matches the barrel markings. Ballistics experts also have electronic and print resources with information on weapons and rifling. They use this collected information to match tiny marks on bullets with those commonly made by various weapons.

The ATF, along with the FBI, maintains a database known as the National Integrated Ballistics Information Network (NIBIN). In the database, categorized information on bullets and shell casings is linked to digital cameras, microscopes, and computers in a system called the Integrated Ballistics Identification System (IBIS). Computer scientists maintain the database and keep improving its search functions to help link spent ammunition to specific weapons and specific weapons to individual suspects.

Police and forensic investigators check bullets recovered from a crime scene to see if they match any other bullets entered into the IBIS system. If an extremely close match is found and the crimes are similar, the likelihood that the bullets were fired from the same weapon is high.

Firearms experts must also determine where the bullet entered and exited an object. This is found by comparing the size of the bullet's entrance hole with the size of the exit hole. Additionally, the exiting bullet will leave a bit of metal on the edges of the hole.

Along with actual parts of weapons and bullets, ballistics experts examine gunpowder residue. This often gives the investigator information about the distance of the shooter from the target when the weapon was fired. The closer to the impacted object, the greater the chance of hot firing gases and bits of gunpowder being spewed onto a victim or impacted object. When a

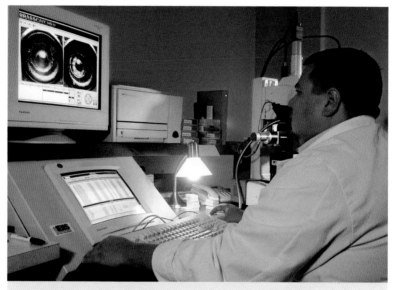

▲ A ballistics expert examines a shell casing on a computer.

weapon is fired at very close range, gunpowder leaves a spatter pattern of tiny black spots around a wound or other impact area. This powder pattern, known as **stippling**, results when burning bits of gunpowder hit skin or an object at high speed and with great heat. The farther away the shooter is from the target, the less chance there is for stippling to occur. In fact, if a suspect claims to have accidentally killed a victim in self-defense while wrestling for a gun, but no stippling is present, the story is considered to lack credibility. If gunpowder residue remains on a suspect's hands, it is no secret that he or she has recently fired a weapon.

A forensic artist
uses clay and a plaster
cast of a skull to
reconstruct the face of
an unknown victim.

CHAPTER FOUR

OTHER AREAS OF
EMPLOYMENT

▼ **FORENSIC SPECIALISTS WHO FOCUS ON** individual criminal traits and motives are important to any criminal investigation. They help fill in potential knowledge gaps of a case and assist police in "reading between the lines" presented by the evidence. Several areas of forensics are central to understanding *why* a crime was committed as well as *by whom* it was committed. These include criminology, psychiatry, and **graphology**. People who work to understand the criminal mind provide crucial tools for information gathering. Understanding why someone commits a crime helps police and forensic investigators find patterns and predict future moves. If a suspect has not been identified, composite artists, working from descriptions provided by witnesses, can produce reasonable likenesses.

▶ CRIMINOLOGISTS

Forensic specialists who study criminal behavior are known as criminologists. They pull together specific details about unknown suspects that will help identify and catch them. This is known as criminal profiling.

Criminals are unique in the ways that they operate. Authorities refer to this way of working as *modus operandi*, or MO. This Latin expression means "the way in which something is done." A criminal profile is compiled with the details of a suspect's MO and anything else that security cameras or witnesses might have noticed. If someone happens to see a tattoo or scar on the robber's arm, that is also recorded.

The profiling process reduces a worldwide set of suspects to a smaller group of people with certain habits and traits. A criminal profile might also be compared to other profiles in other regions. Police often use criminal profiling to predict a suspect's next move and thwart it.

▶ PSYCHIATRISTS

Psychiatrists treat the biological, psychological, and social aspects of mental illness. When analyzing crimes and criminal intent, they try to understand the motivation behind a crime to assist law enforcement in apprehending a mentally disturbed perpetrator. When working with other forensic investigators, psychiatrists provide information on the probable mental state of a dangerous person and try to predict his or her next move. Often this is a challenging task, as many wrongdoers learn from past mistakes, and alter their methods.

A criminal profile is produced by examining subtle clues created during the process of planning, execution, or following a crime. Specifics about the clothes worn, weapon(s) used, victims chosen, sites of crimes, or frequency of criminal activity are also important. A carefully planned and executed crime can be studied by a forensic psychiatrist to learn habits and characteristics of the perpetrator. Information indicating that a crime was committed in haste or in response to changing circumstances or to a victim's reaction also provides clues to the perpetrator's mental state and intent.

The training forensic psychiatrists need to produce a criminal profile in response to crime scene specifics consists of four years of college, four years of medical school, a year of internship in psychiatry, and at least three to four years of psychiatric residency in forensics.

Psychiatrists may also be called upon to decide the mental and legal **competency** of suspects in criminal

THE MAD BOMBER

THE MAD BOMBER, GEORGE METESKY (CENTER),
AFTER HIS ARREST BY NEW YORK CITY DETECTIVES

THE SO-CALLED MAD BOMBER terrorized New York City for over sixteen years, beginning in 1940. His legacy of terror began with a bomb left on a windowsill at the office of the city's provider of electrical power, Consolidated Edison. Although the first bomb didn't explode, the bomber had wrapped a note around it that read, "CON EDISON CROOKS, THIS IS FOR YOU." Later bomb notes were signed "F.P.," but no one could figure out who "F.P." was or why he or she kept planting bombs.

Inspector Howard Finney of the New York Police Department's crime lab was determined to catch the bomber. In desperation, he tried a relatively new technique of psychiatric sleuthing: criminal profiling. He contacted Dr. James Brussel, a psychiatrist, who read the police file and produced the following profile.

The bomber was most likely male, since historically bombers have been male. He was probably a former employee who felt that Con Edison had injured him in some way. He was paranoid, overly sensitive to criticism, and believed that the utility and the public were plotting against him. He was about fifty years old. The bomber's notes, bombs, and planning all showed extreme attention to detail, indicative of someone who was neat and skilled in his work. Brussel also believed that the bomber was born abroad or lived in an immigrant community. Importantly, the bomber lived in Connecticut, since some of the letters had been mailed from Westchester County, which is located between Connecticut and New York. Connecticut was also home to a large number of Europeans.

Con Edison assigned employees to sift through old personnel files looking for someone who fit the bomber profile, and the search produced a match. A former employee named George Metesky of Waterbury, Connecticut, had suffered an on-site accident at the plant where he had worked many years before. Later he had developed tuberculosis, which he thought came from the accident. His disability claim was denied, however, whereupon he wrote angry letters to the company swearing revenge.

George Metesky was arrested, tried, convicted, and sentenced to Matteawan State Hospital for the criminally insane. A model patient, Metesky was released in 1973. He went back to his house in Connecticut where he died at the age of ninety in 1994.

trials. Sometimes a criminal suspect will try to get a lighter sentence by pleading temporary insanity. Psychiatrists evaluate many factors before giving an opinion about whether a person is truly mentally unstable or just pretending. To determine competency, the accused person is interviewed. Reasoning, the understanding of right and wrong, and the ability to feel remorse are evaluated. When people understand the difference between right and wrong, their basic values are in place. If they are not able to see that an act of murder is unacceptable, then deeper mental and social standards are often corrupted as well. If they feel no remorse from criminal actions or do not understand the impact of such behavior on others, they may well act in a similar manner again, since they see no problem with it.

▶ GRAPHOLOGISTS

Graphology is the study of handwriting. For thousands of years, many have believed handwriting can be an indicator of character or personality.

A person's handwriting, like a voice, is individualized. Just as people have different speech sounds and patterns, so do they also have forms of distinct handwriting. However, just as mimics can make themselves sound like another person, so too can forgers copy someone's handwriting well enough to fool the casual

▲ Using a computer, a forensic graphologist compares two handwriting samples.

observer. Graphologists almost always can tell the difference between an authentic signature and a forged one. Art experts often hire graphologists to study art authentication documents to make sure that signatures have not been forged on the art object or its paperwork.

The work of graphologists is also important in resolving cases of check forgery. When a check is signed by someone other than the person whose name is printed on the check, it is said to be forged. The signature is not genuine. Identity theft is a high-tech way of using a person's name and money without permission. Forgery is often an element in identity theft, although today criminals are likely to use illicitly obtained computer passwords or credit card account numbers instead. Graphologists compare genuine examples of a person's handwriting and signature with examples from forged documents to help police catch criminals.

Ransom notes are another area of interest to forensic graphologists. When someone has been kidnapped and family members receive a ransom note, police may consult a graphologist to see what can be learned from the note, especially if no fingerprints were found.

For a career as a graphologist, or handwriting analyst, education is important. Several schools such as the Institute of Graphological Science located in

Dallas, Texas, offer different levels of training and classes in handwriting analysis and questioned-document examination. Founded in 1982, the Institute of Graphological Science was licensed by the Texas Education Agency as the first state-certified graphology school in the United States.

▶ ARTISTS

A forensic sketch artist interviews witnesses and crime victims to gather enough information to produce a drawing that will help authorities in their investigation. Some artists are employed by city police departments, but many do freelance work as independent contractors for several law enforcement agencies. Some forensic artists have Web sites on the Internet to advertise their specialty and provide examples of past work.

The qualifications of a forensic artist vary from a high school diploma to a university degree in criminal justice. Different agencies may also require their own training, but some formal art background is usually required.

Forensic artists are able to transform scanty descriptions into useful investigative tools. Using their imagination and hours of experience in drawing portraits as well as from nature, they are able to

WANTED:
INFORMATION REGARDING THE FOLLOWING INDIVIDUAL AND VEHICLE

The joint task force is seeking assistance from the public in identifying the person in this sketch. This individual has been seen in the area of the shootings that occurred in the Charleston/Kanawha County area during the week of August 10, 2003. Witnesses describe him as a heavy-set, white male, driving a dark colored, full size pickup truck with an extended cab, tinted windows, rear sliding glass window, and possibly a gold or other color stripe around the bottom The truck may be black, dark blue, dark green, or maroon, and is possibly a Ford 150 extended cab pickup truck or similar vehicle.

If you have any information about the above described individual or truck, or if you have **any other information** that you feel might be pertinent to this investigation, contact the task force.

1-866-989-2824 (1-866-WVWATCH)
or
1-304-357-0169

* For an electronic image of this poster, go to www.atf.gov or www.fbi.gov.

▲ A law enforcement poster displaying an artist's sketch of a suspected sniper reproduce crime scenes, recreate facial images from unidentified remains, offer age progressions of victims and suspects from old photos, and generate drawings of suspects' faces from witness descriptions. Additionally, to make a sketch more recognizable, forensic artists must often add personality to a drawing. For example, if a suspect known to be ill-tempered is drawn with a happy smile, many people might fail to recognize the person from the drawing.

Crime scene notes, photos, and other evidence

▼ GETTING TO THE BOTTOM OF A CRIME

is tough, but rewarding. Most people don't experience the daily intrigue and glamour seen on television shows like *CSI: Crime Scene Investigation* or *Bones*. However, working in forensics is an ever-challenging and fulfilling job where good people are appreciated and needed to fill the many professional positions available.

Following every suspicious death or disaster, certain basic questions must be asked to determine whether wrongdoing occurred and if so, to apprehend the perpetrator. Who is the victim? How did the person die? The manner of death is classified as natural, accidental, homicide, suicide, or unknown. For a forensic investigation to be complete, a category must be selected.

▶ FIRST ON THE SCENE

Police officers covering a crime begin their investigation of an outdoor crime scene even before additional officers and medical personnel arrive to examine the body. They set up a crime scene perimeter and are careful to protect evidence. They search the surrounding area for additional victims, suspects, or weapons, and they speak to any witnesses who come forward at the scene.

▲ Numbers mark shell casings at the scene of a shooting surrounded by police tape.

When crime scene investigators and detectives arrive at a home or business, they search the structure, inside and outside, taking note of specifics such as whether windows and doors are open or closed, lights are on or off, and whether odors of, for example, alcohol, smoke, or gunpowder are present. In a home, normal household activities such as a washing machine in use or dinner on the table are recorded. In a business setting, such as an art gallery, a preliminary examination of the alarm system or visual inventory of paintings or sculptures is done.

Documentation of the crime scene through photography, measurements, and sketches helps the legal system retain all the facts of the case. Moreover, after each item has been documented, it is collected, and an evidence **chain of custody** is established. This means that the item is bagged, tagged, and given an identification number. Often crime scene investigators will make unique marks on the item they discuss so that they can know without a doubt when testifying in court that the item they discuss is the same item they collected. Chain of custody clearly identifies who has had possession of the material during various tests and analyses. Evidence must be "checked out" with notes on the time and person requesting the sample as well as when the sample was "checked in" by that person.

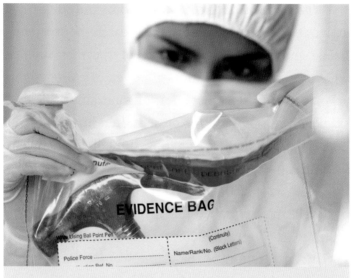

▲ A forensic scientist examines a murder weapon that has been tagged and placed in an evidence bag.

▶ COMING TO A CONCLUSION

The expression "timing is everything" is true in forensic work. Finding out when a crime took place is particularly important, since this information may confirm some suspects' alibis or show that others have lied. Reporting that the victim died during the winter months is generally not good enough for a court of law. Time windows must be narrowed as closely as possible to the suspected time of death. This can be a bit of an art if the body has been buried for months or years. In some cases, of course, witnesses can provide the exact time of death.

Where did the death take place? This can be quite tricky to figure out, especially if the body has been moved from its original location. Finding where a person died or was killed can also be difficult if the victim has been transported by natural forces such as a river. When this happens, only a general location can be stated.

A forensic pathologist makes the final decision in a case. After looking at all the clues provided by examining the body, the pathologist may call for more investigation, such as in a suspected homicide. The case will be closed if the death is found to be from natural causes. However, if the pathologist believes that the evidence is conflicting or yields no clear answer, a death finding of "unknown" is delivered. Just as in determining how a death was caused, a forensic pathologist provides information on the mechanism of death from examining tissues and injuries.

▶ PUTTING IT ALL TOGETHER:
A CASE HISTORY

Sometimes a murder case presents obvious clues. However, what is at first stated as fact may not be true. Such was the case of the seemingly random shooting of Diane Downs's children on the night of May 19, 1983.

Medical personnel were surprised by the tire-squealing, horn-honking arrival of a late-model red Nissan at a hospital emergency room entrance.

CRIME SCENE NOTES

- Date and time 911 call made

- Address of the crime scene and description of the surrounding area

- Weather conditions

- Date and time officers arrived on the scene

- Name and address of person who placed 911 call

- Names and addresses of any witnesses

- Names of officers, forensic investigators, photographers, medical personnel, fingerprint technicians, artists, and anyone else present

- Detailed description of the body and its location within the crime scene

- Detailed description of all evidence discovered at the crime scene

- Detailed description of the crime scene location

- Description of the general area (surrounding buildings, industry, etc.)

- Description of the search pattern used to look for evidence in large spaces, such as fields or wooded areas

- Date and time crime scene investigation ended

• • • • •

As Dr. John Mackey and nurses on duty ran to respond, they were confronted with a blonde woman in her twenties shouting, "Somebody just shot my kids!"

Inside the blood-soaked car, they found one child slumped next to the driver's seat and two other children in the backseat, moaning and gasping for breath. Police were phoned immediately, and while surgeons and teams of medical personnel fought to save the children's lives, police had questions for the young mother, Diane Downs.

A DISTURBING STORY

First the officers wanted to know where the crime had occurred and who had shot the children. In tears, Downs initially told them that on the way home a "bushy-haired stranger" had flagged her down. Thinking he needed help, she continued, she had pulled over and rolled down the window, whereupon the man had produced a gun and demanded the keys. Downs then said that when she refused, he had leaned past her and opened fire on the children. She asserted that she had fought the stranger as he reached for the keys and that he had fired again, hitting her in the arm before she could get the car into gear and speed away, thinking only that her injured children must reach the hospital.

Since the crime had taken place in the Oregon countryside, the Lane County Sheriff's Office became principal investigators. Sergeant Robin Rutherford first spoke with Downs as nurses were tending several small wounds between her wrist and elbow. She said again that she had tried to fight the gunman off. After noticing that the young mother's wounds were minor and that she seemed unusually calm considering the circumstances, Rutherford asked Downs if she would come with him and point out the exact location of the shooting. Downs agreed, and Rutherford was surprised at the dark, desolate spot near the crossing of two roads where the woman said she had chosen to stop for a stranger at night.

Later, back in the hospital, personnel reported that Downs calmly took the news that her middle child had died of her wounds. Then, when told that her three-year-old son had a chance of surviving, she seemed perplexed and asked, "Do you mean the bullet missed his heart?"

Homicide detectives Richard Tracy and Doug Welch interviewed Downs at the hospital and began a time line of events leading up to the shooting.

Downs was a recently divorced postal worker who had transferred from Arizona with the children to be nearer to her parents. The night of the shooting she had visited a friend and taken a shortcut through the country on the way home.

A ballistics report showed that bullets shot at the children were .22 caliber and probably from a handgun. Gunpowder burns on the children's skin indicated that the weapon had been fired at very close range. Blood spatters on the car's windows, doors, and seats pointed to the murderer firing from the driver's side of the car as Downs had described.

THE INVESTIGATORS CLOSE IN

One thing bothered Tracy when he read the doctor's report of Diane Downs's arm injury. Apparently one bullet had entered her left forearm, split into two when it hit the bone, and then exited, leaving two small wounds. Tracy noted that the injury was similar to those past killers had inflicted on themselves in trying to make it look as though they had been attacked.

Criminalists arranged for Downs's car to be transported to the crime lab, and the body of Downs's seven-year-old daughter to be sent to the **morgue**. Bloody clothing from the three children had been collected from the hospital emergency room and sent to the forensic lab for analysis. Pathologists reported that tissue analysis and gunpowder residue indicated that the shots that had killed one child and critically injured her siblings had been inflicted at extremely close range.

The first time Downs was allowed to see her surviving daughter, aged eight, nurses reported that the woman's "I love you" had been spoken in an icy tone between clenched teeth. An investigator present at the time noted the little girl's expression of fear at her mother's approach. The heart monitor jumped over 40 beats per minute when Downs took the little girl's hand.

When questioned, Downs admitted to owning a .22 caliber rifle and a .38 caliber pistol. Detectives who searched her home and car found the guns, but neither had been fired recently. The search for the .22 caliber handgun went on for months, covering every inch of the crime scene, including the nearby river. However, .22 caliber shell casings matching casings found in Downs's car were recovered from the area. They were of the same caliber as shots that killed one child and injured the two others. Upon testing, they were found to have been fired by the same gun.

In an interview with Detective Welch in Arizona, the children's father, Steve Downs, stated that Diane Downs owned three guns, the .22 caliber rifle, the .38 revolver, and a .22 caliber Ruger Mark IV nine-shot, semi-automatic pistol. He told how Diane used to practice at the local firing range for protection on her mail route. This last clue pointed a finger squarely at Diane, since she had failed to tell the police about the third gun.

Steve also described an affair Diane had while still in Arizona following their divorce. The man was married and worked with Diane at the post office. Though the man had broken up with Diane, she was obsessed and continued to call and write him. After a final rebuff, Diane took the kids and moved to Oregon. Further interviews with fellow postal employees and babysitters painted a picture of a woman who put everything and everyone ahead of her children.

THE TRUTH IS REVEALED

Fred Hugi of the district attorney's office was assigned to prosecute the case. As more and more details of Diane Downs's life came to light, Hugi was less and less inclined to believe the woman's story about an unknown shooter that dark night. How did the shooter know she was going to be there? Was he waiting for her and, if so, how did he get in front of her car as she had reported? If the man had wanted only the car, wouldn't he shoot Downs instead of the small children? Guards were assigned to keep a twenty-four-hour watch over the two children recovering at the hospital.

Further examination of Downs's car raised more questions. If Downs had been in the car when the shooter fired the shot that reportedly had hit Downs in the arm while she was struggling with her assailant,

▲ Convicted murderer, Diane Downs

why had forensic investigators found no blood on Downs's other hand, the one she'd used to grab her wounded arm, or on the steering wheel? No powder marks from the shooter's gun were found on the driver panel or anywhere on the driver's side of the car. Investigators deduced that whoever did the shooting was seated in the driver's seat and that Diane Downs had shot herself just prior to arriving at the hospital.

Trace evidence aside, nothing is more powerful than eyewitness testimony. In the end, the forensic clues and analysis supported what Diane Downs's young daughter told the jury at the trial a year later: her mother shot her sister, then leaned over the seat and fired at her and her little brother. Diane Downs was sentenced to life in prison.

▼ GLOSSARY

accelerant a substance used to increase the speed with which a fire spreads

adipocere a waxy gray to brown substance that is created as fat decays during decomposition of a body

autopsy the examination and dissection of a corpse to determine the cause of death

ballistics the study of what occurs when a firearm is fired

botany the study of plants and their structure

chain of custody the system of keeping track of who has had possession of evidence from the time of its collection at a crime scene throughout its various tests and analyses and as it travels from labs to offices to courtrooms

competency the ability to perform mental and physical tasks at standard established levels

criminalistics the study of crime, criminals, criminal behavior, and corrections

DNA (deoxyribonucleic acid) the protein that makes up the genetic building blocks of all living organisms

forensic science the scientific study of crime scene evidence

forensics the art or study of debate; often related to forensic science

graphology the study and interpretation of handwriting

homicide death caused by or at the hand of another; murder

medical examiner (ME) a public official who performs autopsies

morgue hospital lab facility in which autopsies are performed

odontology the study of teeth and dental composition

postmortem the time after death has occurred

projectile a thrown, fired, or otherwise propelled object, such as a bullet

rifling spiral grooves along the inside of a gun barrel that help stabilize the bullet as it exits the barrel at high speed

rigor mortis the slow stiffening of muscles after death

serology the study of bodily fluids such as blood, tears, saliva, semen, and urine

shrapnel bits of a projectile, often metal, that are thrown out from an explosion

stippling pattern of tiny black spots of gunpowder around a wound or other impact area caused when burning bits of gunpowder hit skin or an object at high speed and high heat at close range

toxicology the study of the nature, effects, and detection of poisons

trace evidence small particles of materials such as hair, paint, glass, soil, and fibers that can serve as clues in an investigation

▼ FIND OUT MORE

BOOKS

Douglas, John. *Careers in the FBI*. New York: Simon & Schuster, 2005.

Platt, Richard. *Crime Scene: The Ultimate Guide to Forensic Science*. New York: Dorling Kindersley, 2003.

Saferstein, Richard. *Criminalistics: An Introduction to Forensic Science*, 8th ed., high school version. Upper Saddle River, NJ: Pearson Education, 2004.

WEB SITES

www.aafs.org/default.asp?section_id=resources&page_id= choosing_a_career
American Academy of Forensic Sciences

www.cci.ca.gov/about/aboutcci.htm
California Criminalistics Institute

www.handwriting.org/
Handwriting analysis

www.trivia-library.com/c/detective-edward-o-heinrich- and-the-mail-train-murders-part-2.htm
Mail Train Murders

▼ BIBLIOGRAPHY

Books

Cole, Simon. *Suspect Identities: A History of Fingerprinting and Criminal Identification.* Cambridge, MA: Harvard University Press, 2003.

Evans, Colin. *The Father of Forensics: The Groundbreaking Cases of Sir Bernard Spilsbury and the Beginnings of Modern CSI.* New York: Berkley, 2006.

Fisher, Barry, et al. *Forensics Demystified.* New York: McGraw-Hill, 2007.

Galton, Francis. *Finger Prints.* Originally published in 1892. Amherst, NY: Prometheus Books, 2006.

Inman, K., and N. Rudin. *Principles and Practices of Criminalistics.* Boca Raton, FL: CRC Press, 2001.

Innes, Brian. *Bodies of Evidence.* London: Amber Books, 2000.

James, Stuart H., and Jon Nordby. *Forensic Science: An Introduction to Scientific and Investigative Techniques.* Boca Raton, FL: CRC Press, 2002.

Libal, Angela. *Forensic Anthropology.* Brookmall, PA: Mason Crest, 2006.

Saferstein, Richard. *Criminalistics: An Introduction to Forensic Science,* 9th ed., college version. Upper Saddle River, NJ: Prentice Hall, 2007.

Temple, John. *Deadhouse: Life in a Coroner's Office.* Jackson: University Press of Mississippi, 2005.

WEB SITES

www.atsdr.cdc.gov/MHMI/mmg8.html
Agency for Toxic Substances and Disease Registry, Division of Toxicology, U.S. Department of Health and Human Services. Public Health Service: Atlanta, GA

www.crimelibrary.com/index.html
Crime Library: Criminal Minds and Methods

www.minddisorders.com
Psychiatry educational requirements and training

www.payscale.com/research/US/Job=Forensic_Science_Technician/Salary
Forensic Science Salaries

http://wtc.nist.gov
National Institute of Standards and Technology (NIST), Federal Building and Fire Safety Investigation of the World Trade Center Disaster

▼ INDEX

▼ ABOUT THE AUTHOR

LINDA D. WILLIAMS is a nonfiction writer with specialties in science, medicine, and space. Ms. Williams's work has ranged from biochemistry and microbiology to genetics and nanotechnology. She has worked as a lead scientist and technical writer for NASA, McDonnell Douglas Space Systems, Rice University, and the University of Arkansas for Medical Sciences.